I WANT TO BE . . . Book Series
Creator/Producer: Stephanie Maze, Maze Productions, Inc.
Writer and Educational Consultant: Catherine O'Neill Grace
Designer: Alexandra Littlehales

Photographers for I WANT TO BE A FASHION DESIGNER:
Nicole Bengevino, Chuck Fishman, Andy Levin,
Richard T. Nowitz, Lara Jo Regan, Barbara Ries, Tom Story

Other books available in this series:
I WANT TO BE AN ASTRONAUT
I WANT TO BE A CHEF
I WANT TO BE A DANCER
I WANT TO BE AN ENGINEER
I WANT TO BE A FIREFIGHTER
I WANT TO BE A VETERINARIAN

Library of Congress Cataloging-in-Publication Data
Maze, Stephanie.
I want to be a fashion designer/created and produced by Stephanie Maze;
Catherine O'Neill Grace, writer and educational consultant.
p. cm.—(I want to be—book series)
"A Maze Productions book."
Summary: A photo-essay introducing career possibilities
within the fashion industry and describing how to get an early start
pursuing a career in this field.
ISBN 0-15-201863-8 ISBN 0-15-201938-3 (pb)
1. Costume design—Vocational guidance—Juvenile literature.
2. Fashion designers—Juvenile literature.
[1. Costume design—Vocational Guidance. 2. Fashion designers.
3. Vocational guidance. I. Grace, Catherine O'Neill, 1950– .
II. Title. III. Series.
TT507.M382 2000
746.9'2'023—dc21 98-38506

First edition
C E F D B
A C E F D B (pb)

Film processing by A & I Color, Los Angeles
Pre-press through PrintNet
Printed and bound by Tien Wah Press, Singapore

I Want to Be...

A FASHION DESIGNER

A Maze Productions Book

HARCOURT BRACE & COMPANY

SAN DIEGO   NEW YORK   LONDON

ACKNOWLEDGMENTS

We wish to thank the following people, companies, and institutions for their very valuable contributions to this book: Oscar de la Renta; Bill Blass; Patrick Robinson; Eduardo Lucero; Amsale Aberra; Liz Claiborne; Tommy Hilfiger; Josie Cruz Natori; Kenneth J. Lane; Adam Lippes; Saks-Jandel of Chevy Chase, Maryland; Fashion Institute of Technology; Council of Fashion Designers; Hard Candy; Avirex; Esprit; Patricia Underwood; Adriana Caras; Judy Caliendo; John Roberts; Zazu and Violet's Hats; Jesse Mononogya; Levi Strauss; the Washington Opera; Glenna Johnson H_2O Silks; MAGIC International; Cultural Mission of the Royal Embassy of Saudi Arabia; Information Center of the Embassy of the Republic of Korea; Library of the Embassy of India; Information Center of the Embassy of Nigeria; Dover Publications; Josef's Hair Salon of New York; Calm Creations; Wristies; Janney Elementary School; Franklin Middle School; Los Angeles Fashion Career Center High School.

Many thanks, also, to all the professionals in this book for allowing us to interrupt their busy schedules and for agreeing to be the wonderful role models children can look up to for many years to come.

To all children who dream the impossible dreams

Where to Start

Do you love clothes? Do you spend hours planning your outfits? Do you like to sketch ideas for dresses, suits, or hats? Do you enjoy sewing your own apparel? Are you a fan of fashion magazines? If so, you may have the imagination and flair it takes to become a fashion designer.

People wear clothes primarily as protection from the elements. But once you're covered up, you start to think about how the clothes look on you and what they say about you. Clothes express your individuality. They may show what culture you belong to and they can tell others how you like to spend your time. (Think of the flowing saris worn by women in India, or a Boy or Girl Scout uniform.)

Fashion is a reflection of who we are and the times we live in. It is the display of popular tastes—and tastes change all the time. When you look at a garment you may say, "That's in fashion" or "That's out of fashion." Designers like Bill Blass (left), one of the legends of American fashion, can be important trendsetters.

Blass, who was born in Indiana in 1922, works in New York City, the center of the American fashion industry. For decades his haute couture—one-of-a-kind high-fashion garments—has influenced American style. Blass was among the first designers to adapt menswear styles for women and he is well known for his comfortable sportswear. But above all, he says, "I love making evening clothes." He designs simple but elegant gowns, such as this gorgeous red-and-purple evening ensemble worn by model Irina Tortchinskaia. That's fashion!

Types of Designers

Fashion designers work in a variety of capacities, from serving apprenticeships with established high-fashion houses to heading their own small companies.

Young designer Patrick Robinson, shown in the large photo on the facing page, started out working for respected fashion leader Anne Klein, and later, Giorgio Armani, but he soon struck out on his own. He has already achieved great success. When he showed his first *line*—a collection of his own designs—at the New York fall fashion shows in 1995, he was only twenty-eight.

Robinson usually works with a neutral color palette of gray, ivory, and black, accented by splashes of orange and red, and he uses all kinds of fabric—including synthetics that look like metal. Influential buyers who purchase clothing to sell in their stores visit Robinson's New York City *atelier*, or "workshop," to snap up his well-tailored collection.

Clothes may be the foundation of fashion, but accessories can be just as important. The right shoes, handbag, hat, or jewelry can make an old garment look fresh and up-to-date.

Creativity abounds in the field of accessory design. Jesse Monongya—a well-known Native American jewelry maker who works in Phoenix, Arizona—uses gold and precious stones to put a contemporary spin on traditional Navajo-style jewelry (top right).

Jeweler

Handbag designer

Handbag happy. *Designer Adriana Caras looks over her most recent collection in her Los Angeles, California, studio (above). Her handbags are inspired by old-time Hollywood and the glamour of 1960s fashion figures. Her work is popular with young Hollywood stars.*

Head to toe. Influential New York hat designer Patricia Underwood trims the brim of a felt hat (far left). She's also known for fun straw creations. In Los Angeles shoe designer Birgit Klett, who works for Esprit, makes sketches as she redesigns details of a sneaker (near left).

Milliner

Shoe designer

A Fashion Show with Oscar de la Renta

Each spring during "Fashion Week" in New York City, leading designers present their collections of clothing for the fall season. In each show dozens of models walk proudly down the runways wearing the designers' most recent creations for the hundreds of buyers and clients in the audience, as well as for reporters and photographers from trend-setting magazines. The photos on these pages, including the one above, take you to Oscar de la Renta's fall 1998 fashion show.

Born in the Dominican Republic, Oscar de la Renta started his fashion career as a staff designer in Spain for Balenciaga. He later founded his own fashion house in New York. Fashion critics consider de la Renta one of the most important American designers. He specializes in

luxurious, dressy clothes for formal occasions.

Staging a fashion show is a big production—like putting on a play! Backstage, dressers help models make lightning-quick changes from one outfit to another so there's no break in the action on the runway. Music plays. Lights flash. For a grand finale, there's often a bridal gown.

De la Renta's fall show took place under a large tent in Bryant Park, in New York City (large photo, left). Every detail, from the models' hair to the color of their stockings, had to be just right. De la Renta admits he's a perfectionist!

The collection was a smashing success with the crowd—and the fashion press. After the show a favorite client congratulated de la Renta on his new collection (far right, bottom).

Are you struck by the designer's bold use of form and color, such as the crimson dress modeled by Esther Cañadas (near right)? De la Renta originally planned to become an abstract painter but, instead, decided to apply his artistry to clothes. "The cut and color of clothes are very important to me," de la Renta has said. "Also, I love to combine different textures."

Supporting cast. A fashion show requires the teamwork of many people, including makeup artists (small photo, facing page), hairdressers (above left), and dressers (above center), who help models make quick changes and assemble the outfits listed on a "sequencing" chart (above right). A videographer records the action (below).

Education

Would you like an early start on a fashion career? Some elementary and high schools take fashion seriously. They offer kids classes to sharpen their design skills and give them hands-on experience with fabric, color, and *merchandising*—the process through which products are designed, developed, marketed, and sold.

At Janney Elementary School in Washington, D.C., students in a fourth-through-sixth-grade art class learn to coordinate colors and patterns and to paint on fabric—some of the skills involved in textile design (large photo). In the photograph at bottom right on the facing page, a Janney student works on an image he will eventually transfer onto a piece of cloth.

In Los Angeles, California, interested eighth graders can apply to the Fashion Career Center High School, a magnet public high school that specializes in teaching fashion skills—from designing, fashion illustration, and pattern making to manufacturing, merchandising, and retailing. They also find out that there's more to fashion than making sketches and putting together outfits. Students do internships in stores to understand the retail end of the fashion business. At left, Paola Gudiel learns how to display accessories at CalMart, a California apparel center with more than one thousand showrooms. One hundred and ten students enroll in the program each year. Almost all of the graduates go on to college to study fashion.

Hands-on training. *Fashion Career Center High School student Valerie Godbold drapes fabric around a mannequin as she designs an evening gown (above). Draping allows her to see what a garment will look like and to start putting together the pieces of a pattern.*

Good for them. *At Franklin Middle School in Chantilly, Virginia, students stitch stuffed animals (above) to donate to nursing homes. According to the Home Sewing Association's research, sewing enhances creativity and problem-solving skills.*

Fashion Institute of Technology

The Fashion Institute of Technology takes up a whole block on Seventh Avenue, right in the heart of America's fashion capital, New York City. FIT, as it's called, is part of the New York State University system. It offers courses in art, design, technology, and business to prepare students to enter the fashion industry.

Founded in 1944, FIT offers courses in more than thirty fields that relate to fashion and design. In the large photo above, FIT students in a fashion illustration class learn to sketch from a live model. Every year some twelve thousand students pursue a range of degree programs, from a one-year associate degree to bachelor's or master of arts degrees.

If you ask FIT students what they're studying, the answers will vary widely. You might hear "fabric styling" or "international trade and marketing for the fashion industry," "packaging design" or "cosmetics and fragrance marketing." The students working with bottles and jars in the photo at right center are learning how to make fragrances and perfumes.

Fashion design students at FIT learn fashion history, pattern making, and computer-aided design (top right). They work with leading designers who visit the college each semester to comment on their work. Some of the visitors, such as designers Norma Kamali, Calvin Klein, and Jhane Barnes, are famous FIT graduates. Students of apparel design may concentrate on tailoring menswear (small photo, facing page), or designing clothing for children (below), among several other specialties.

The students get lots of hands-on experience with real companies. For example, FIT fashion design students redesigned the New York City Transit Authority's employee uniforms.

Some fashion-loving kids can't wait until college to get started. That's why FIT also offers a wide range of popular "Saturday Live" classes, just for high school students; subjects include fashion illustration for beginners, sewing for fashion designers, computer basics for designers, and the business of fashion.

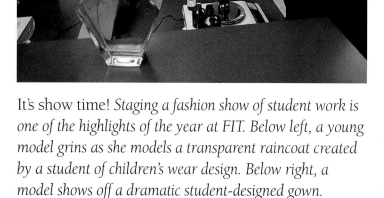

It's show time! *Staging a fashion show of student work is one of the highlights of the year at FIT. Below left, a young model grins as she models a transparent raincoat created by a student of children's wear design. Below right, a model shows off a dramatic student-designed gown.*

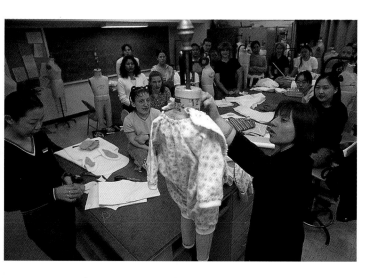

Ready, set, sew! *Learning to make outfits at home is fun for sister and brother Lauren and Justin Williams (above). Lauren makes some of her own outfits. Justin enjoys making small stuffed animals, which he gives to his friends as gifts.*

Other Programs and Experience

You don't necessarily need to go to a special school to plunge into the world of fashion at an early age. On these pages kids sew, silk-screen, and model clothes for fashion experience. Lauren Williams, eleven, and Justin Williams, thirteen, operate sewing machines under the watchful eye of their mom, Laura Williams (large photo). "They love making toys and other little things," says Laura. "Once they get on the machine, they want to try everything." Laura, who began sewing at age nine, makes many of the children's clothes herself. She also teaches young people to sew in her Washington, D.C., home. "Sewing is an important practical skill and can be a money saver," she says. "If you have a big family and you're on a budget, making clothes can be cost-effective—and you get better quality."

In the small photo at far left, youngsters learn how to silk-screen images onto T-shirts in a summer class at the Corcoran School of Art in Washington, D.C. The gallery offers hands-on experience in the arts, which nurtures the creativity and sense of design that kids will rely on if they choose a career in fashion.

Walking down a runway may look easy, but it's not! Models learn special ways of standing, turning, and walking to display the features of the clothing they wear. Child models in a Fashion Institute of Technology show (near left) walk with confidence and style.

Fashion Vocabulary

The fashion industry has many facets—including design, manufacturing, and merchandising—and each has its own distinct language. People in the fashion world use the words and terms on these pages to talk about their business.

COMPUTER-AIDED DESIGN (CAD)

With the help of CAD, or "computer-aided design," fashion professionals such as this designer at Liz Claiborne, Inc., design everything from textile patterns to whole lines of clothing more easily. Special software programs allow designers to see their ideas in a variety of color combinations and to create templates that can be sent directly to a factory to be cut out and produced. CAD lets designers preview designs without creating actual samples.

PANNIERS

Many different kinds of structures have been used over the centuries to define the lines of clothing. These panniers were constructed to shape the voluminous skirt of a costume to be worn on stage at the Washington Opera. But in the eighteenth century, fashionable women wore structures like this under their clothing every day to shape the big skirts they wore! Panniers are named after twin baskets that are slung over an animal's back or a person's shoulders.

PIPING

The milliner working on this straw hat is measuring its crown to determine the amount of piping—or decorative finishing ribbon—that will be needed to adorn the hat and finish off its raw edges. Piping is also applied to clothing as decoration, as well as to prevent seams, hems, and other fabric edges from unraveling. Piping is only one of many types of decorative trimming that can be applied to hats or clothing as a finishing detail.

SCENT STICK

A student of perfume manufacturing at the Fashion Institute of Technology sniffs a scent stick as she selects ingredients for a distinctive aroma. Perfumes are made of combinations of natural and synthetic oils and fragrances. This student might be sampling attar of roses, sandalwood, or the scent of some other flower or spice. Many fashion designers produce signature colognes, such as Coco Chanel's Chanel No. 5 and Calvin Klein's Obsession.

CROQUIS

Croquis (pronounced crow-kee) are rough sketches in which artists note preliminary ideas for various designs. The sketches are used to develop many kinds of products. Here, a designer for the sportswear manufacturer Esprit compares a croquis of a platform shoe to a sample of the design.

CUTTER'S MUST

A cutter is a person who cuts out garment pieces for production. In factories, cutters may use power saws or other electric machinery to trim around pattern pieces. In couture houses, they painstakingly cut out each piece by hand. A detailed set of instructions put together by the designer—called a cutter's must—indicates exactly how to cut out the pieces.

SHEATH

A sheath is a dress that skims along the body. The garment hangs from the shoulders with some shaping, but it does not have a tight, fitted waist. Sheaths were made popular in the 1960s by former First Lady Jacqueline Kennedy, who wore them at formal and informal occasions. The comfortable dresses have become trendy again in the 1990s.

MANNEQUIN

A mannequin is a model of a human form. Designers and seamstresses use the forms when they drape patterns or tailor clothing. Some couturiers keep mannequins made to match their clients' measurements so they can custom-make garments for them. The figures are also used to display clothing in a showroom or in a store.

SHOWROOM

Customers and buyers can visit a designer's showroom to view a collection up close and to try on garments. Sometimes fashion shows or fittings are held there as well. Here, young designer Eduardo Lucero prepares for visitors, adjusting a gown on a mannequin in his showroom in Hollywood, California.

SPOOLS

Huge spools of brightly colored fiber fill these bins in a textile factory. These spools of thread will soon be attached to machinery that will weave the fibers together on huge looms and produce fabric. Computer-aided manufacturing, or CAM, has streamlined textile production. But human beings are still needed to set up the looms.

A Designer at Work

Judy Caliendo (above) designs clothes for John Roberts, a women's wear company located in New York City's busy garment district. She specializes in creating evening clothes for a collection called JR Nites, which is sold in department stores throughout the United States. In the photos on these pages, Judy and her assistants work on their fall 1998 collection.

"I start by making a quick sketch," Caliendo says. "I get ideas from fashion reports, from constant shopping, from new fabrics, from what people are wearing in the streets. Most artists get ideas from practically anything!"

When Caliendo finishes a sketch, an assistant cuts it out in muslin and drapes it over a mannequin (above top). When the look seems right, a paper pattern is cut using the muslin pieces as guides (facing page, top right). Caliendo also selects colors for the outfit (above bottom).

Following the pattern, a seamstress makes a single sample of the garment (facing page, bottom left) in the chosen fabric. The selection of trimmings, such as buttons, completes the process (below center).

The final test comes when a live model tries on one of Caliendo's designs (below right). "You need to look at it on a human being instead of a mannequin," says Caliendo.

Once she sees how the piece fits, Caliendo can make final adjustments to details, such as hemlines. "When I see a sample finished and it looks the way I thought it should—that's the best part of my day," she says.

Once a sample is just the way Caliendo wants it, the pattern for this garment is sent to a factory, where machines produce many copies of it in a variety of standard sizes. And at last the garments arrive in department and specialty stores throughout the country, to be sold.

One of the best parts of her job, Caliendo says, is when she catches a glimpse of one of her designs on a customer at a wedding or evening event. "It's just great to see that the dress or blouse or gown we worked so hard on looks so nice and that someone is enjoying wearing it."

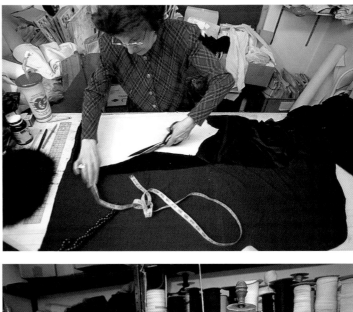

Putting it together. *A seamstress pins the muslin pieces of a pattern on a mannequin for correct sizing and fit (above). Designer Judy Caliendo may then make adjustments on the piece—a tuck here, a hem there, perhaps even a different collar.*

The History of Fashion Design

The drawing at left depicts an artist's idea of what Stone Age fashion might have looked like. Human beings have clothed their bodies for protection since prehistoric times. Archaeologists have even found evidence of ancient "fashion" in cave paintings.

A simple form of clothing called a loincloth, shaped somewhat like a diaper, made way for a variety of draped clothing in the ancient world. The Egyptians, Greeks, and Romans developed methods of weaving fibers into fabric that could be easily draped (pictures, top right). Ancient peoples decorated their clothing, with patterns such as the designs on the robes of the Greek women in the sketch at second from top, right.

Europeans borrowed Roman styles well into the fifth century A.D. In the colder climates of northern Europe, people wore belted tunics with trousers or leg banding. European dress changed very little until the fourteenth century. Then clothing became more ornate as better fabrics—especially silks and brocades—arrived in Europe from the Middle and Far East. Clothes began to be tailored to the body, influenced by the Italian Renaissance, with its emphasis on the beauty of the human form. The button, an innovation imported from the Middle East, helped to make clothes fit better.

Toga party. *Rome is famous for the toga (top right), a piece of material draped around the body. The toga was a mark of distinction; only Roman citizens could wear it.*

Tunic time. *For many centuries, European fashion was based on simple tunics and robes, whether for French ladies, peasants, or knights of the Middle Ages (above, left to right), or Dutch nobility of the early Renaissance (right).*

As the centuries progressed, aristocratic clothes became more elaborate. In the sixteenth century, men began wearing stockings, called hose, along with tunics of very rich cloth—perhaps even embroidered in gold, if you were an important person like King Henry VIII (above left). In the seventeenth century, aristocratic women all over Europe often wore ruffs of lace, made fashionable by England's Queen Elizabeth I (second from left). By the eighteenth century, aristocratic clothes had become even more grandiose (above, second from right). Nineteenth-century women favored corsets that created a small waist, set off by skirts shaped by a hooped petticoat (near right).

But by the end of the eighteenth century, fashion had returned to simpler roots. Women began to wear flowing—and undoubtedly more comfortable—styles reminiscent of Roman robes. The two ladies at top right wear Empire gowns popular in the early 1800s. Chic men's clothing in the mid nineteenth century included tight frock coats and shiny top hats (far right, second from top).

In the late nineteenth century, industrial developments revolutionized the fashion world,

Casual and dressy. *Sports became chic in the 1900s, so women began wearing practical outfits including bloomers (right, second from bottom). Gowns by Worth, a Paris couturier, were the rage for ladies in Europe and the United States (bottom right).*

Sew your own! *American Elias Howe (above), who lived from 1819 to 1867, perfected sewing machines, changing the face of fashion.*

New trends. *In the early 1900s shorter hemlines radically changed women's fashion. The hobble skirts designed by Paul Poiret and Erté (top left and second from left) soon gave way to the even shorter 1920s flapper style (above, second from right).*

New looks. *In the 1940s American Claire McCardell invented comfortable sportswear for women (left). In Paris, Christian Dior introduced his "New Look"— princess-line skirts and coolie hats (above).*

making stylish clothes more accessible and creating a new genre of apparel for the active lifestyles of the industrial era. Inventions such as the bicycle, the automobile, and the sewing machine all played roles. To ride bicycles safely, women needed free movement of their legs, so they began wearing baggy pants. People called these *bloomers,* after American reformer Amelia Bloomer, who believed in women's rights—and wore trousers herself. Skirts shortened and narrowed as women began to travel by car. Children's clothes became more practical as did men's suits (above, far right). And thanks to the invention of the sewing machine and the increased availability of patterns, practically anyone could wear high fashion.

By the twentieth century, fashion had become big business and designers began to be recognized as famous personalities. Poiret, Balenciaga, Schiaparelli, Lanvin, Chanel, and Dior became household names. And celebrities such as the Duchess of Windsor (above left, second from top), who wore a pale blue Mainbocher gown when she married the Duke of Windsor, set fashion trends. Coco Chanel (left, second from bottom) perfected simple, elegant suits for women

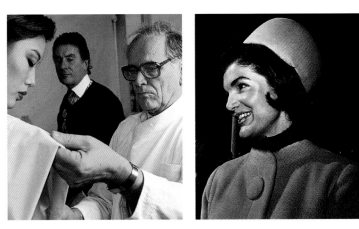

and invented the classic perfume Chanel No. 5.

In the 1960s First Lady Jacqueline Kennedy (above, second from left) dramatically influenced fashion. American women mimicked her sense of style. A hat like her pillbox, for example, designed by Halston, became a must-have item for every chic woman. Pierre Cardin (top left) became the first designer to put his name on everything from clothes to luggage. Yves Saint Laurent (above, second from right) had a huge impact on fashion with his pantsuits and peasant dresses. Youth fashion—including the miniskirt (top right) introduced by British designer Mary Quant—also took the world by storm in the sixties and seventies.

In the 1980s and 1990s, big-name designers such as Ralph Lauren created classic American looks with tweedy suits and elegant sportswear (center right, second from top). In Italy, Giorgio Armani (center right, second from bottom) started a rage for elegant tailoring and luxurious fabrics that quickly spread worldwide. And the work of avant-garde designers including Issey Miyake of Japan and Jhane Barnes of the United States made fashionable people begin to look ahead to the twenty-first century.

Innovation. *Japanese designer Issey Miyake encourages freedom of movement with his beautifully cut, easy-flowing clothes (below).*

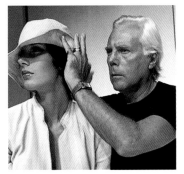

Hall of fame. *Designers (above, left to right) Alber Elbaz, Isaac Mizrahi, Oscar de la Renta, Todd Oldham, Anna Sui, Donna Karan, Calvin Klein, and Byron Lars gather in New York in 1992.*

Computing creativity. *At Liz Claiborne, Inc., a New York City company that designs and markets a wide array of women's and men's apparel, designer Martha Friend uses a computer-aided design (CAD) system to work on a line of sportswear. She draws with a stylus on a digitizing pad connected to her computer. CAD programs can assist designers in sketching, creating textile designs, or pattern making. The software allows designers to envision their ideas without having to physically create patterns and samples. Computerized patterns can be sent directly to manufacturing.*

Technology

Ever since the sewing machine revolutionized fashion in the mid nineteenth century, designers and manufacturers have been adapting technology—especially computers—to assist them in their businesses.

Computer-aided manufacturing, or CAM, is especially useful in the development and manufacturing of textiles. Not only are textile patterns designed on computers, the new technology is used to figure out weaving sequences and to run machinery. That results in cheaper, faster, and more streamlined fabric manufacturing, which allows for more economically produced clothing.

At top left, a worker gets ready to attach a spool of thread to computerized machines that will weave it into fabric. At center left, a technician uses computerized equipment to test the strength of various parts of a piece of fabric.

Some experimental designers have incorporated computers right into outfits, creating "wearable technology." At bottom left, a woman models what people might wear in 2007. The outfit, called Lingua Trekka, includes a vest that carries an ambient linguistic device—a portable translation system. Microphones are embedded in the front neckline; speakers are located in the back. A mini screen and keyboard provide Internet access. You can't buy this outfit—yet. Only one exists, designed by students from Japan's Bunka Fashion College in Tokyo for the Massachusetts Institute of Technology's annual international design seminar.

Menswear magic. *At the annual "Magic Show" in Las Vegas, seventy thousand buyers and sellers gather. They can check out everything from Hawaiian shirts to chic winter jackets (above left and right) amid hundreds of stalls displaying men's clothing.*

Trade Shows

Can you imagine a convention hall filled with feathers, buttons, and bows for trimming outfits and hats, like the feather headdress at left, designed by Larissa Aranda. How about hundreds of Hawaiian shirts or scores of winter jackets like those shown on the facing page? That's what buyers, retail store owners, and in some cases the general public find when they attend events called trade shows. There the people who make apparel and accessories meet the buyers—store owners and other retailers who select merchandise to sell in stores. The shows offer designers and manufacturers an opportunity to present their wares in an effort to get them placed in stores around the country.

Every major city in America and many foreign countries stages bridal fairs, special trade shows where prospective brides and grooms can peruse a vast selection of wedding gowns, bridesmaids' dresses, tuxedos, and all the necessary—and sometimes not-so-necessary—wedding accessories. In the large photo on the facing page, models prepare for a fashion show at a bridal expo in Milan, Italy.

Trade shows occur nearly every month in cities from San Francisco, California, to New Delhi, India. They bring together people interested in products ranging from old-fashioned straw hats to high-tech textiles. One of the largest trade shows is the International Fashion Boutique Show held in New York City, where thirty-five thousand fashion professionals gather!

Taking an order.
At the International Children's Fashion Trade Show at the Javits Center in New York City, buyers can browse through some sixteen hundred lines of boys' and girls' clothing. Above, a buyer makes a deal with two salespeople to purchase girls' dresses from a children's apparel line called Radish Bunch. A deal like this can mean a successful season for a small company.

International Attire

Designers often seek inspiration for their work in the rich traditions of clothes from around the world. All of the traditional costumes on these pages are still worn today—some as everyday wear, some for ceremonial purposes. Do these styles inspire you to set a new fashion trend?

HANBOK. Korea's traditional garment has not changed for two thousand years.

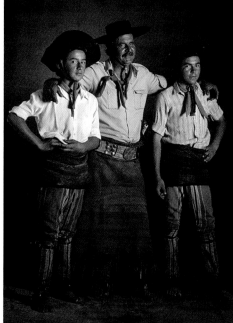

BOMBACHAS. These brightly striped pants are worn by gauchos in Argentina.

TUNICS. These jackets are worn by the Royal Canadian Mounted Police.

CASSOCK. A Catholic priest's red robe shows he's a cardinal, or church leader.

SCHOOL UNIFORM. Straw hats and blazers identify these Australian students.

DJELLABA. Moroccan men wear this traditional flowing white cotton robe.

PUKU. A Sami man in Lapland wears a tunic of reindeer hide.

PARKA. An Inuit family bundles up in fur-lined hide tunics that protect them from the harsh Arctic environment.

IBO and **BUBA**. Traditional Nigerian headdress and shawl

ÁO DÀI. The traditional garment for women in Vietnam

THOUBE. Saudi Arabian men wear this long robe.

KILT. A Scot wears a skirt in his family's tartan, or plaid.

SARI. This graceful silk robe is worn by women in India.

KIMONO. Japan's chosen garment since the seventh century

MILITARY UNIFORM. Worn by U.S. Marine cadets, this uniform has barely changed since the 1800s.

SAFFRON ROBE. Buddhist monks in Asia wear this garb.

Did You Know . . .

. . . that there are thousands of different kinds of fabric, ranging from alpaca, a soft material made from the hair of camel-like animals living in the Andes mountains, to velvet, a lustrous woven fabric with a short, dense pile and a rich texture. Textile artist Glenna Johnson, of Washington, D.C., chooses to work with silk, a delicate natural fabric that drapes nicely. She hand painted the beautiful one-of-a-kind fabrics—which include silk, satin, chintz, velvet, and chiffon—displayed in the photo at left.

. . . that human beings began using sewing needles as early as 10,000 B.C.? The "eyes" of prehistoric ivory and bone needles were most likely threaded with animal tendon to piece together garments made of skin or fur.

. . . that in the late nineteenth century, people wore long, baggy woolen tunics and knickers as bathing suits? The first formfitting elastic swimsuit didn't come along until 1920.

. . . that the leotard was worn first by a nineteenth-century French trapeze artist? His name? Jules Léotard.

. . . that Benjamin Franklin invented suspenders—or *gallowkes,* as they were called at first—back in the 1730s? They were an official part of the uniform worn by firefighters in the nation's first volunteer fire department, which Franklin founded.

. . . that sneakers were originally called croquet shoes? They've been popular since the 1860s. In 1917 U.S. Rubber introduced one of the most popular sneaker brands, Keds. The name combines *kids,* the audience the company hoped to capture, and *ped,* the Latin word for *foot.*

. . . that Levi's jeans are named for miner Levi Strauss, who invented them during the California Gold Rush in the 1850s. He made the first Levi's out of brown tent canvas. Later he began using a tough cotton fabric called denim, dyed blue with indigo. He placed metal rivets at the points of strain on the pants so they would wear better. Levi Strauss took out a patent on his durable pants in 1872. His descendants are still making blue jeans.

Related Careers

You don't have to design clothing to affect the way people dress. Buyers like Dina Garber can influence the fashion world. Buyers visit showrooms and fashion shows to select the clothes that will sell in retail stores throughout the United States. Some buy ready-to-wear clothing in large quantities to sell at big department stores; others buy for small boutiques.

Garber specializes in purchasing small quantities of clothes from high-end designers. Her selections will be sold at Saks Jandel, an upscale women's clothing store in Chevy Chase, Maryland, near Washington, D.C. In the large photo on the facing page, she inspects the quality of a pair of pants from a recent fall collection. The clothes she chooses for the store can influence fashion trends in her region. It looks like tan will be in this year!

Modeling is another exciting way to step into—and sometimes to shape—the fashion world. At lower left, a young woman who hopes to become a model reviews a portfolio of her portraits with a fashion photographer. Perhaps she will become one of the next "supermodels" on the covers of influential magazines or in clothing ads. Supermodels' styles of hair, makeup, and clothing often set fashion trends for a season or two.

Behind the scenes. *You could choose a career as a costumer. At the Washington Opera in Washington, D.C., Anna Keyser repairs the elaborate costumes that were designed for* Rigoletto *and Cinderella (above center). Textile inspectors, like the man at right above, make sure new fabrics are free of defects. Well-made fabrics are the beginning of any truly snazzy piece of clothing.*

Artistry. *Makeup artist Todra*
Payne applies eye shadow to model Oluchi (left)
A stylist tries out color palettes (above).

Definitions of cool. *Hard Candy nail polish was the brainstorm of Dineh Mohajer (above left). The now-successful cosmetics maker was a college student when she decided she needed blue nail polish to go with some blue platform shoes—and a huge fad was born. Love of vintage airplanes and airplane gear led to a business for Jacky and Jeff Clyman (above right). Since 1975 their company, Avirex USA, has been producing classically cool American leather flight jackets, favorites of celebrities including actor Sylvester Stallone and singer Puff Daddy.*

Entrepreneurs

The fashion world attracts creative people with new ideas. On these pages, you'll meet some entrepreneurs—people who organize, operate, and assume the financial risk for their own business ventures—whose individualized "looks" have energized fashion.

In the large photo on the facing page, Mexican American designer Eduardo Lucero puts together a colorful outfit in his trendy Hollywood, California, shop, which is also called Eduardo Lucero. He creates a variety of designs for famous clients and for his store, including Latin-inspired bright, billowy tops and formfitting jeans reminiscent of the pants worn by Spanish flamenco dancers.

At right, Jamaican textile designer Claudette Lopez Byer of Washington, D.C., works on a sample of the one-of-a-kind painted fabric she uses for her line, CALM Creations. Byer transforms plain silk, cotton, hemp, and wool into vivid tropical scenes—"Nature inspires me," she says. Then Byer sews the fabrics into kimonos, camisoles, and sarongs for sale in boutiques.

Wedding belle. A bride stands still as Ethiopian-born designer Amsale Aberra adjusts her veil (right). A graduate of the Fashion Institute of Technology in New York City, Aberra started out by designing and making her own bridal gown. She opened her bridal business six months later. Aberra began her career in Manhattan, where she recently launched an evening-wear line that has attracted the attention of Hollywood stars such as Kim Basinger and Vanessa Williams.

Fine shoemaking. *Italy has long been known for its handmade shoes. After all, the ancient Romans were the first shoemakers to develop shoes shaped accordingly for the left and right foot. In the small photo below, two shoemakers who work near Milan use traditional methods to attach heels to shoes.*

Craftsmanship around the World

Fashion designers often look to the fabrics, special products, and craftsmanship in different parts of the world for inspiration and guidance. Some countries are well known for certain products and processes, including China for luxurious silks (facing page, top right), France for precious perfumes (below center), and New Zealand for the finest quality Merino wool (below right).

In the large photo at left, a Nigerian woman practices an age-old African craft: a special method of dyeing fabric, called batik. To batik, she covers a piece of cotton in a pattern of wax. The cloth is then soaked in dye. Because the wax resists the dye, the cloth emerges embla-zoned with a colorful pattern. Multicolored patterns can be made by repeating the dyeing process several times over. Batiking is especially prevalent in Southeast Asia as well as in Africa.

Perfume making is another hands-on craft that is associated with a specific region of the world. In the center photo below, a perfumer is shown filtering a mixture of flowers and oils to extract the precious essence, or scent, of the blossoms. She works in Grasse, a town in south-eastern France that is the center of the country's perfume industry. Roses, jasmine, and other flowers used to make perfumes grow in the vicinity, making the countryside around Grasse an inspiring place to visit—and to smell!

Carnaval! *In Rio de Janeiro, some seamstresses specialize in creating the elaborate beaded, sequined, and frilly costumes that people wear for the joyous celebration just before Lent (above left).*

How Silk Is Made

Ready to hatch. Workers must keep an eye on the silkworm larvae (right) and gather them up when they seem ready to emerge.

It all starts with worms. That's right—silkworms! Silk comes from the cocoons (small photo, far left) spun by silkworms that later metamorphose into the Bombyx mori moth. Silk production, or sericulture, is a complex process that requires caring for the worm from the egg to the pupal stage—and many, many mulberry leaves, because that's all these silkworms eat.

Silkworm caterpillars form their cocoons by producing a long fiber called a filament. They do this by giving off, or secreting, a liquid through the spinneret—a tube in the head. The secretions harden to form filaments. Each cocoon contains filaments that together can add up to a fiber two thousand to three thousand feet long!

In the large photo on the facing page, Chinese workers sort silk cocoons according to shape, size, and color. They free the filaments by softening the cocoons in water. Then they unwind, or *reel*, the filaments from several cocoons at the same time. The fragile silk strands that result are twisted together to make skeins of thicker thread (bottom right). These threads can be woven into the beautiful, lustrous, and surprisingly strong material we call silk.

According to Chinese records, the process of silk production was developed around 2700 B.C. Chinese legend tells of a prince who told his wife to examine the silkworm and test the practicality of using the thread. She determined how to raise silkworms, how to reel the silk, and how to weave it and sew it to make garments. This princess was later honored with the name "the Goddess of Silk Worms." The methods of silk production were kept secret by the Chinese for about three thousand years. Those methods then spread to other parts of the world.

Munch, munch. *Some silkworms (above) feed only on mulberry leaves for twenty-three days. Workers (below) stay busy supplying the hungry creatures! Then the worms begin to spin cocoons out of sticky secretions from glands inside their bodies.*

Softening the silk. *When they are mature, cocoons are boiled to soften the filaments of silk that form them (right). While the cocoons are still damp, silk workers unwind the long, delicate strands onto reels by hand. The strands can be spun into silk threads.*

Other Famous Designers

Sometimes fashion designers are so influential that their work brings about fundamental changes in fashion. The creativity and flair of the designers on these pages has changed the way people dress.

PAUL POIRET
This French couturier was the most fashionable dress designer in the first two decades of the twentieth century. He was the first to shorten skirts!

GIANNI VERSACE
Inspired by his sister Donatella, Italian designer Versace created luxurious, formfitting, ultramodern clothes. He also began lines of menswear, fabrics, and furniture, and he occasionally turned his hand to costume design for the Italian opera. When Versace died in 1997, his sister took over as lead designer.

HUBERT DE GIVENCHY
Shown here with his "muse," actress Audrey Hepburn, French designer Givenchy is famous for the elegance and graceful lines of his couture.

KENNETH J. LANE
This American artist made costume jewelry fashionable. His elegant, fun, and well-made work uses imitation jewels and metals that keep his designs affordable.

HELENA RUBENSTEIN
Born in Poland in 1870, this cosmetician came to the United States after World War I and founded Helena Rubenstein, Inc., a leading women's beauty product company.

VERA WANG
Acclaimed for her wedding gowns, Wang brings simplicity and elegance to bridal wear. Before starting her own line, she was a senior fashion editor at *Vogue* magazine.

LILY DACHE
Hers was a household name in the 1930s and 1940s, when women wore hats every day. The milliner set fashion trends by creating glamorous headwear for movie stars.

KARL LAGERFELD

This German designer, based in Paris, has been influential in the 1980s and 1990s. He has created looks for six different high-fashion houses, including Chanel and his own KL. His bright colors and bold lines bring wit to traditional fashion.

JOSIE CRUZ NATORI

The founder and head designer of the Natori Company began her professional life as an investment banker but soon left that industry to start her clothing business. Her line, which originally featured lingerie and sleepwear, has expanded to include day and evening wear.

MISSONI

The Missoni family of Milan, Italy, is well known for colorful patterned knitwear for men and women. In the 1960s the Missonis' success helped establish Milan's annual fashion week.

ANNE KLEIN

This inventor of "separates"—different pieces that can be combined to create many outfits—focused on the needs of working women.

EDITH HEAD

This movie costume designer, who died in 1981, worked on a thousand films and won more Oscars than any woman in Hollywood history.

TOMMY HILFIGER

The Hilfiger sportswear "look" is popular with all ages—from teenagers to rap stars and sports figures. In 1998 he added housewares, including towels and sheets, to his best-selling line.

KANSAI YAMAMOTO

"I am making happiness for people with my clothes," this Japanese designer has said. He creates clothes that bring Asian traditions, such as the bold shapes of Japanese Kabuki theater costume, to Western-style dresses and suits.

SALVATORE FERRAGAMO

This footwear designer, a master craftsman who lived from 1898 to 1960, was one of the world's most innovative shoe designers. He transformed the look and fit of the shoe, creating more than twenty thousand styles in his lifetime, including the popular spike high heels.

You Can Be a Fashion Designer

Has this book sent you scurrying to your closet to take a closer look at your wardrobe? Have you started sketching ideas for clothes you'd like to make or textiles you'd like to design? Fashion inspiration can come along suddenly, as fourteen-year-old K-K Gregory, of Bedford, Massachusetts, found out when she was only ten.

"One day there was a big snowstorm and that night I was outside building a fort with my brother and my wrists were bothering me," K-K recalls. "My mom came out and said, 'Look at you! You have snow all over your mittens and half up your sleeve. Why don't you go in and sew something to fix that?'"

That's how Wristies—K-K's successful design for fingerless fleece hand protectors—got started. Wristies go up the arm and stop below the elbow. Worn with gloves, they offer extra protection from snow and ice.

K-K used Polartec fleece to sew up her first few pairs. She tried them out on members of her Girl Scout troop, and they were an instant hit. "Make more!" her friends demanded. K-K did, and in the four years since then she has sold Wristies on television's Home Shopping Network and through a well-known national mail-order catalog. She's running a thriving business, which includes a website (www.wristies.com) from which people can order her invention. Wristies are popular with rock climbers, mail carriers, marching-band members, garbage collectors, and—of course—kids who play in the snow.

"I never imagined that I could invent something that would become a whole company," says K-K. "Some kids don't realize they have good ideas. They can start their own business with a simple good idea."

Other Sources of Information

FASHION ORGANIZATIONS:

American Apparel Manufacturers Association
25500 Wilson Blvd.
Arlington, VA 22201

The members of this group produce approximately 80 percent of the clothing sold in the United States. They also provide consumers information about clothing.

Childrenswear Marketing Association
236 Route 38 West, Suite 100
Moorestown, NJ 08057

This national trade group represents manufacturers and suppliers of children's clothing in the United States.

Costume Designers Guild
13949 Ventura Blvd., Suite 309
Sherman Oaks, CA 91423

A union of costume designers employed in the motion picture and television industry.

Council of Fashion Designers of America
1412 Broadway, Suite 2006
New York, NY 10018

Members of this group are well-known designers. The council conducts the Costume Institute at the Metropolitan Museum of Art in New York City.

The Fashion Association
475 Park Avenue South, 9th Floor
New York, NY 10016

This association promotes fashion and retail to the media.

International Association of Clothing Designers
475 Park Avenue South
New York, NY 10016

An organization of well-known men's and women's fashion designers.

National Textile Center
2207 Concord Pike
Wilmington, DE 19803

NTC is a research consortium of six universities: Auburn University, Clemson University, Georgia Institute of Technology, North Carolina State University, the University of Massachusetts-Dartmouth, and the Philadelphia College of Textiles and Science. Its mission is to provide research and support for the U.S. textile industry.

A SELECTION OF PROFESSIONAL FASHION SCHOOLS:

Fashion Institute of Technology
Seventh Avenue at 27th Street
New York, NY 10001

This world-renowned college in New York City offers degree programs in the art, design, business, and technology of fashion.

Parsons School of Design
66 Fifth Avenue
New York, NY 10011

This college's mission is "to educate the leadership of tomorrow's art and design communities." Parsons offers a major in fashion design.

Philadelphia College of Textiles & Science
School House Lane
and Henry Avenue
Philadelphia, PA 19144

Founded in 1884, this was the first textile school in the United States. it offers degrees in textile design, fashion design, and textile and apparel manufacturing.

Massachusetts Institute of Technology (MIT)
Media Laboratory
77 Massachusetts Avenue
Cambridge, MA 02139

MIT includes the Media Lab that sponsors an annual wearable technology symposium.

A SELECTION OF FASHION MUSEUMS

Bata Shoe Museum
327 Bloor Street West
Toronto, Ontario
Canada M5S IW7

Housed in a building reminiscent of a shoe box, this museum houses the world's largest collection—more than 10,000 shoes dating back 4,500 years.

The Costume Institute
The Metropolitan Museum of Art
1000 Fifth Avenue
New York, NY 10028

This museum of fashion history has a comprehensive permanent collection as well as regular exhibitions, and publishes books about fashion.

Kent State University Museum
Kent State University
Kent, OH 44242

Nine galleries at this university museum feature exhibitions of fashion and the decorative arts.

Museum of Fine Arts, Houston
The Textiles & Costume Institute
1001 Bissonnet at Main
Houston, TX 77005

The institute's collection was founded in 1986 to stimulate public awareness of costume as an art form and to provide a visual history of costume.

MAGAZINES, NEWSPAPERS, AND FASHION PUBLISHERS

Conde-Nast Publications, Inc.
350 Madison Avenue
New York, NY 10017

This company publishes many influential fashion magazines, including Allure, Brides, Details, Glamour, GQ, and Vogue.

Daily News Record (DNR)
7 West 34th Street
New York, NY 10001

This trade newspaper covers all aspects of the menswear and textile industries.

Dover Publications, Inc.
31 East 2nd Street
Mineola, NY 11501

This company publishes a wide variety of historical fashion catalogs and pattern books.

Threads
63 South Main Street
Box 5507
Newtown, CT 06470

This magazine is designed for knitters, sewers, fabric and textile designers, and craftspeople.

Women's Wear Daily (WWD)
7 West 34th Street
New York, NY 10001

This trade newspaper covers all aspects of women's fashion.

FASHION TRADE SHOWS

The Larkin Group
100 Wells Avenue
Newton, MA 02159

This company owns and manages three of the fashion industry's largest and most successful trade show events: the International Fashion Boutique Show, the International Kids Fashion Show, and the International Fashion Fabric Exhibition.

MAGIC International
6200 Canoga Avenue, Suite 303
Woodland Hills, CA 91367

This organization runs men's, women's, and children's apparel trade shows. Its biggest is the annual "Magic Show," the largest men's and general apparel market, which attracts 80,000 members from 105 countries twice a year.

MODELING ORGANIZATIONS

Elite Model Management Corp.
111 East 22nd Street
New York, NY 10012

The company manages top fashion models.

Ford Models, Inc.
142 Greene Street
New York, NY 10012

The agency manages top fashion models, including child models.

Model Search America (MSA)
588 Broadway, Suite 711
New York, NY 10012

Every year this group conducts 250 regional searches for new models in the United States and Canada. Major modeling agencies in both countries are members of MSA.

PHOTO CREDITS